For Stephanie, Caleb and Kyndra.
I love you all so much.
Always be yourself and make a positive difference.

Order this book online at www.trafford.com
or email orders@trafford.com

Most Trafford titles are also available at major online book retailers.

© Copyright 2012 Cal Davis.

All rights reserved. No part of this publication may be reproduced, stored in a retrieval system, or transmitted, in any form or by any means, electronic, mechanical, photocopying, recording, or otherwise, without the written prior permission of the author.

Printed in the United States of America.

ISBN: 978-1-4669-0296-1

Library of Congress Control Number: 2011919836

*Trafford rev. 01/19/2012*

Trafford
PUBLISHING  www.trafford.com

North America & international
toll-free: 1 888 232 4444 (USA & Canada)
phone: 250 383 6864 • fax: 812 355 4082

# I'm Just a Crow

Written and Illustrated by Cal Davis

I'm just a crow.
Just an ordinary crow
--nothing special.
And I live the usual
boring life of a crow.

Nobody likes us.
We are never invited to the bird parties.

We crows are so unloved.

We are always getting chased away…

...or scared off.

We must hide when we eat because Old Farmer Brown gets angry at us when we dine in his yard.

I wonder how it would be if I was not a crow. Hmm. What could I be?

How about a cat? Cats get to lie around all day and sleep. And they don't have to hide when they get their food.

Cats play all the time and don't have to work like we crows do.

But wait! Cats are around people!
I don't like people.
I'd rather be a bird.

Why can't I have beautiful colors like other birds?

A snowy owl. Now that's cool. Actually, that's too cold. I don't think so.

Now that's beautiful. Being a swan would be wonderful. They don't work and only show off their beautiful feathers. But I don't want anyone watching me.
Maybe a swan isn't the bird for me.

What about a roadrunner? I could run really fast away from Old Farmer Brown. He'd never catch me! But I sure would get tired. I'd rather fly. No, not a roadrunner.

Woodpecker? Oh, what a headache!

Ostrich? Nope, too big.

Hummingbird?
Way too small.

How about a turkey? Just walk around and eat all day. What a life! At least until Thanksgiving! Ouch!

"Come to think of it, if I was another bird, I couldn't play games with my crow buddies. We crows love to play games.

I guess the best thing for me to be is…

…ME!

An elementary teacher by degree, Cal Davis is happily married to Stephanie and they have two wonderful children, Caleb and Kyndra, and make their home in Texas. Cal is a veteran, a Boy Scout, and a Gideon. He is involved in church and his community as well as state organizations.